Published By Robert Corbin

@ Leif Hopkins

Making Pizza: Easy Recipes to Make Pizza at

Home for Beginners

All Right RESERVED

ISBN 978-87-94477-03-1

TABLE OF CONTENTS

Sesame Seed Bread 1

"Stout" Bread 4

Italian Pizza Margherita.. 7

Pizza From Puff Pastry With Mushrooms...................... 10

Beef Taco Salad Pizza 12

Best-Ever Buffalo Chicken Pizza 15

Pepperoni Pizza On The Grill... 18

Italian Pizza «White-Green».. 20

Thin Crust 22

Portobello Mushroom Crust 23

Italian Riviera Pizza Mini-Pizza Muffins.......................... 24

Ham And Cheese Mini-Muffins 28

Grandma Pizza.. 30

Regina Pizza 32

Barbecue Pizza 34

Basil And Three Cheese Thin Crust Pizza....................... 35

Keto Pepperoni Pizza... 39

- Keto Pizza Chicken Recipe 41
- Gluten Free Pizza With Figs, Feta And Kale Pesto 43
- Sweet Italian Sausage Gluten-Free Pizza 47
- Pizza With Spinach, Red Onions, Mushrooms, And Pepperonis 49
- Pizza With Green Olives And Basil 53
- Creamy Salmon Shirataki Fettucine 56
- Creamy Mussel With Shirataki 59
- Garbanzo-Onion Bread 62
- Onion And Poppy Seed Bread 65
- School Pizza 68
- Closed Pizza 70
- Best-Ever Homemade Pizza 73
- Blackberry Ricotta Pizza With Basil 77
- Pizza Bianca 81
- Bbq Chicken Pizza 83
- Pizza On The Grill Pan 85
- Pizza Margarita In The Grill 87

Eggplant Parmesan Slices 90

Rosemary, Feta Cheese And Dried Tomato 92

French Riviera Savory Herb And Bourse Mini-Muffins... 95

Marguerite Pizza 97

Marinara Pizza 99

Blackberry Brie Pizzettas 101

Breakfast Pizza 104

Keto Pizza Chicken.. 106

Keto Pizza Crust - Plain Chicken 109

Three Cheese Pizza... 111

Quinoa Pizza Crust.. 115

Grilled Onion And Cheese Pizza 118

Beef-Asparagus Shirataki Mix 121

Garlic-Butter Steak Bites With Shirataki Fettucine 124

Pizza From Puff Pastry With Lecho............................... 127

Fruit Pizza 129

Mini Pizza Eggplant 131

Broccoli-Bacon Skillet Pizza Recipe 133

Butternut Squash Pizza & White Sauce, Spinach, & Goat Cheese Recipe 136

Capricious Pizza 139

Fruited Brownie Pizza 141

Italian Pizza On The Home Grill 143

Homemade Pizza 145

Pizza With Seafood 147

Sesame Seed Bread

Ingredients:

- 170 g sesame seed flour

- 57 g flaxseed

- 2 tablespoonsful of sesame seeds, lightly roasted

- 2 teaspoonful of baking powder

- Xanthan gum, 1 table spoon

- 3 eggs (150 g)

- ¼ cup (57 g) unsweetened soy milk or other milk of choice

- Few drops of liquid stevia

Directions:

1. Warm up the oven to 3700F.
2. Grease the baking tray with oil and you can as well line the base of the pan with a parchment paper.
3. In a mixing bowl, pour in the sesame flour, sesame seeds, flaxseed flour, xanthan gum, baking powder, and desired quantity of salt. Mix the ingredients properly.
4. Mix the rest of the wet ingredients in a separate bowl thoroughly.
5. Combine the dry and wet mixture for few minutes to make a sticky dough.
6. Once you're satisfied with the consistency, pour the mixture, into prepared pans filling them till it is 1 inch away from the top.
7. Bake large loaves for 20-25 minutes, turn the other side of the loaf and bake for another 20-25 .

8. When the bread appears brown and fluffy at the centre, turn off the heat.
9. Let the bread cool a little in the pan for about 10 minutes but just before you turn out the loaf.
10. Allow the loaf to cool on the wire rack for about 15 minutes before slicing.

"Stout" Bread

Ingredients:

- 1 teaspoon xanthan gum)

- 4 eggs (200 g)

- 1 cup (230 g) unsweetened soy milk or other milk

- 1 cup (230 g) water

- ½ cup (120 g) salted butter or margarine, melted

- Salt

- 2 cups (230 g) garbanzo bean flour

- 1 cup (120 g) golden flaxseed meal

- ½ cup (80 g) flaxseeds

- ¼ cup Splenda or Stevia Extract

- 4 teaspoons baking powder

- Powdered black pepper

Directions:

1. Warm up the oven to 3700F.
2. Grease the baking tray with oil and you can as well line the base of the pan with a parchment paper.
3. In a mixing bowl, pour in the dry ingredients which includes garbanzo flour, flaxseed flour whole flaxseed, xanthan gum, sweetener, baking powder, salt and pepper as desired. Mix thoroughly.
4. In a separate container, or preferable an electric mixer, mix the milk, water, eggs, butter till a thorough formulation is achieved.

5. On medium speed combine the dry and wet mixtures for about 5 minutes till a well-aerated, sticky dough is achieved.
6. Transfer the flour mix into the greased baking tray.
7. Bake for about 35 minutes, turn the other side of the dough and bake for another 35 minutes till a toothpick or knife comes out lean from the centre of the loaf.
8. Let the bread cool a little in the pan for about 10 minutes just before you turn out the loaf.
9. Allow the loaf to cool on the wire rack for about 15 minutes before serving with your desired soup or stew

Italian Pizza Margherita

Ingredients:

Dough:

- 2 tsp dry yeast (6 g)
- 1/2 tsp salt
- 1 cup warm water
- 2.5 cups flour
- 2 tbsp. olive oil

Filling:

- 5 tomatoes, scald, remove the peel, coarsely chopped
- 75 g of brine mozzarella cheese, cut into slices
- 6 basil leaves, torn

- Salt, pepper, olive oil

Directions:

1. In a bowl sift the flour, make a small depression and pour into it the oil, add the yeast and salt pour a glass of warm water.
2. Put the dough on a work surface and knead until it is elastic - about 10 minutes.
3. Cover and let the dough come in a warm place for 30-60 minutes (we were in a hurry; you can leave for 3-4 hours).
4. I came up in the dough multicooker with the lid closed; I did a pre-warmed on the heating and switched off.
5. Preheat oven to 210 C. Baking grease or put the parchment.
6. Roll out the dough into a large circle on a floured table, transferred to the pan.
7. Spread the dough chopped tomatoes, drizzle with olive oil.

8. Bake for 15-20 minutes, then add the slices of mozzarella and basil, salt and pepper, drizzle with oil again and return to the oven for another 7-8 minutes.

Pizza From Puff Pastry With Mushrooms

Ingredients:

- 200 grams of mushrooms (frozen)
- Vegetable oil for frying
- 500 g of cooked sausage
- 150 g of cheese
- 250 g puff pastry
- Flour for rolling out dough
- for the sauce: ketchup, mayonnaise, cheese sauce
- 7 eggs

Directions:

1. Heat oven to 200 C. Roll out the dough.

2. Lubricate sauce.
3. Mushrooms fry in vegetable oil.
4. Put the stuffing: sausage + mushrooms + cheese grated + grated egg. Put the pizza in the oven.
5. After 25-30 minutes to get ready-made pizza.

Beef Taco Salad Pizza

Ingredients:

- 1 flour tortilla 12" flour tortilla
- 1 1/2 cup shredded cheddar divided
- 1 cup shredded romaine
- 1/4 cup sour cream sour cream
- 1 tomato diced roma tomato
- 1 1/2 tablespoon olive oil extra-virgin olive oil divided
- 8 ground beef oz. lean ground beef
- 1 packet seasoning taco seasoning
- salt kosher salt
- black pepper Freshly ground black pepper

- 1/2 avocado avocado thinly sliced

Directions:

1. Preset the oven to 400º. Lightly grease a new baking sheet together with 1/2 tablespoon olive oil make aside.
2. Inside a skillet, put the remaining tea spoon oil and dark brown the beef, three to four minutes.
3. Add follón seasoning and carry on and brown until gound beef has cooked by means of, 4 to a few minutes more.
4. Softly season with sodium and pepper.
5. Spot tortilla on a new greased sheet pan in addition to top with .5 cup cheese. Leading cheese with gound beef mixture and one more 1/2 cup parmesan cheese.
6. Bake until parmesan cheese has melted as well as the tortilla has crisped up, 7 in order to 8 minutes.

7. Eliminate from oven plus top with leftover cheese, shredded lettuce, sour cream, tomato vegetables, and avocado. Function.

Best-Ever Buffalo Chicken Pizza

Ingredients:

- 1/2 teaspoon garlic powder

- 2 cups shredded cooked chicken

- 8 ounces ball mozzarella, torn

- 1/3 cup blue cheese , crumbled

- 1/4 red onion , thinly sliced

- 1 pound . Pizza dough, divided in half

- Cornmeal , for pan

- 4 tablespoons butter

- 1/4 cup hot sauce (such as frank's), plus more for drizzling (optional)

- 2 green onions , thinly sliced

Directions:

1. Preheat oven to 500°. Brush two big baking sheets along with vegetable oil plus sprinkle each along with a layer associated with cornmeal.
2. Place chausses in a moderate microwave-safe bowl.
3. Microwave until melted, twenty to 30 mere seconds.
4. Whisk in very hot sauce and garlic clove powder until mixed.
5. Pour half associated with the buffalo spices over chicken plus toss to coating.
6. On a gently floured surface, condition each half associated with pizza dough in to a round golf ball, then press over the center of every to produce a 1/2" brown crust area.
7. Using the dough relaxing around the back associated with your hands as well as your knuckles, gently extend dough out with the

aid of gravity by shifting your hands in . by inch together the crust.

8. Move to prepared cooking sheets.
9. Add fifty percent of the leftover buffalo sauce in order to each pizza plus spread all around the money (leaving the exterior 1" bare).
10. Divide sauced chicken, torn mozzarella, blue cheese, plus red onion equally between the pizza. Bake pizzas till crust is fantastic and cheese will be melty, 15 in order to 17 minutes.
11. Ornament with green onions and a drizzle of hot spices (if using) plus serve immediately.

Pepperoni Pizza On The Grill

Ingredients:

- Frozen pizza dough 400 g
- Pizza sauce 50 g
- Mozzarella cheese 100 g
- Pepperoni 100 g

Directions:

1. Place the stone base.Prepare pizza on the grill over a divorced fire.
2. Roll out the dough to the desired thickness. Then shift to the stone base for cooking.
3. Keep over the heat for 10 minutes until Golden.
4. Remove from heat. Apply the sauce in a thin even layer.

5. Sprinkle mozzarella cheese evenly to the center of the pizza. Then lay out the pepperoni slices.
6. Return the pizza to the fire, raw side down. Cover with foil and cook until the cheese melts-10 minutes.

Italian Pizza «White-Green»

Ingredients:

- 20 g finely grated parmesan
- 2 handfuls of young arugula (with small stems and leaves)
- A half of a lemon
- Olive oil
- 1 pizza dough piece (radius about 30 cm)
- 100 g. Fresh mozzarella
- Salt

Directions:

1. Heat the oven as much as possible. Break up mozzarella and distribute on the extended test.

2. Drizzle with olive oil and salt. Sprinkle with Parmesan on top.
3. Bake until the crust is Golden and the cheese melts (about 10 minutes).
4. Pour the arugula with olive oil in a separate bowl, salt and lemon juice.
5. Once the pizza is ready, decorate with arugula and serve.
6. Very tasty Italian pizza, the simplest recipe and fast cooking.

Thin Crust

Ingredients:

- 1 Low-Carb Flour Tortilla
- Sauce, Cheese, & Toppings of your choice
- Olive Oil

Directions:

1. Preheat oven to 450F.
2. Brush slightly with olive oil.
3. Place in oven for 1 to 2 minutes to harden and toasted.
4. Remove from oven and add the sauce.
5. Add cheeses and toppings of your choice.
6. Cook for an additional 3-6 minutes or until cheese is melted.
7. Serve hot. Enjoy!

Portobello Mushroom Crust

Ingredients:

- 4 tbsp Olive Oil
- Sauce, Cheese, Toppings of choice
- 2 large Portobello Mushroom

Directions:

1. Preheat oven to 350F.
2. Scrape out the innards of the mushrooms and continue scraping the meat out until you are left with just the mushroom shell.
3. Coat mushrooms with about olive oil.
4. Broil mushroom shell for about 5 minutes.
5. Fill with Sauce, Cheese and Toppings.
6. Bake for 10-15 minutes or until cheese has melted and starts to brown.
7. Serve hot. Enjoy!

Italian Riviera Pizza Mini-Pizza Muffins

Ingredients:

- 1 teaspoon sugar or sugar substitute of your choice
- 1/4 teaspoon fresh garlic, minced
- 1/4 teaspoon salt
- 1/3 cup low-fat milk, or soy or other milk of your choice
- 1/3 cup feta cheese, crumbled
- 1 large egg, well beaten
- 2 tablespoons tomato paste
- 1/3 cup pepperoni, finely chopped (optional, leave out for vegetarian)
- 2 tablespoons extra-virgin olive oil

- 2/3 cup purple or white onion, finely chopped

- 1/3 cup red bell pepper, finely chopped

- 1/3 cup yellow bell pepper, finely chopped

- 1/3 cup whole-wheat pastry flour

- 1/3 cup all-purpose flour

- 2 teaspoons baking powder

- 1 1/2 teaspoons fresh oregano, chopped

- 1/2 teaspoon dried dried oregano

Directions:

1. Preheat oven to 180 degrees Celsius (350 degrees Fahrenheit)
2. Heat olive oil in a large frying pan over medium heat. (You want the oil to be shimmering, but not smoking.)
3. Add onion and red and yellow bell peppers and garlic; saute, stirring often, until the onion

is tender, and garlic is fragrant, about 5 minutes.
4. Transfer to a large bowl and let cool for about 10 minutes.
5. Coat your mini-muffin cups with olive oil (if not non-stick)
6. In a large bowl, whisk together flours, baking powder, oregano, sugar, garlic powder and salt.
7. Make a small well inside the center of the dry mixture.
8. Now add the milk, egg, tomato paste and into the onion mixture. Stir to combine. Add crumbled feta, fold in again gently.
9. Add the wet Ingredients:into the dry ones and stir until just combined. It's okay to have lumps and pieces of dry Ingredients:.
10. If you're using pepperoni, fold it in now, and stir once or twice to add to mixture.

11. Carefully spoon the muffin mixture into the mini-muffin cups, about two-thirds full.
12. Bake the muffins until lightly browned, approximately 10 to 12 minutes. (A toothpick inserted into the center of a muffin comes out clean.)
13. Let the muffins cool for about 5 minutes before removing from pan and putting on wire rack till cool.
14. Cool in the pan for 5 minutes before turning out onto a wire rack.
15. Serve warm or at room temperature.

Ham And Cheese Mini-Muffins

Ingredients:

- 100g (3.5 ounces) Parmesan cheese, slivered or grated

- 200g (8 ounces) frozen corn kernels (optional)

- 2 eggs

- 150g (4 ounces) salted butter

- 125ml (1/2 cup) milk

- 125g (1/2 cup) self-raising flour

- 100g (3.5 ounces) favorite ham, finely diced

- 100g (3.5 ounces), mild Cheddar cheese, grated

- 100g (3.5 ounces) sharp Cheddarcheese (or hard cheese of your choice), finely grated

Directions:

1. Preheat oven to 180 degrees Celsius (350 degrees Fahrenheit)
2. Mix all Ingredients:together until just combined in a large bowl.
3. Grease your hands with olive oil, and roll 'apricot sized' balls and place one in each mini-muffin cups.
4. Bake for between 10 -12 minutes in pre-heated oven or until they are golden brown and spring back when lightly touched in the middle.
5. Remove from muffin cups and cool on wire rack.

Grandma Pizza

Ingredients:

- 3/4 cup pizza sauce

- 2 1/4 cup shredded mozzarella cheese

- 1 teaspoon dried oregano

- 2 tablespoons extra-virgin olive oil

- 2 ounces thinly sliced mushrooms

- 3 ounces sliced pepperoni

Directions:

1. Preheat oven to 300°F.
2. Drizzle a 13-by-18-inch rimmed baking sheet. Cook cream cheese keto crust as stated above until crust is golden brown.
3. Remove crust from the oven and increase oven temperature to 450°F.

4. Spread baked keto crust with olive oil and pizza sauce.
5. Sprinkle with mozzarella, top with mushrooms and pepperoni, and season with oregano.
6. Bake for 10 minutes. Slice and serve.

Regina Pizza

Ingredients:

- 2 cups shredded mozzarella cheese
- 1 sliced tomato
- 1 ounce sliced black olives, drained
- 1 teaspoon dried oregano
- 1/3 cup your favorite pizza sauce
- 2 cups thinly sliced fresh mushrooms
- 1 1/2 cups chopped ham

Directions:

1. Place sliced mushrooms in a small microwave-safe bowl.

2. Microwave on high power until mushrooms are tender (for 2 to 3 minutes). Drain mushrooms.
3. Cook cream cheese keto crust as stated above.
4. Remove crust from the oven and increase oven temperature to 450°F.
5. Spread baked keto crust with pizza sauce and sprinkle with oregano.
6. Add the tomato, mozzarella, ham, mushrooms, and olives.
7. Bake until cheese is melted. Serve hot.

Barbecue Pizza

Ingredients:

- 2 pound shredded or chopped barbecue pork
- 1/2 cups (6 oz.) shredded Monterey Jack cheese
- (12-inch) prebaked pizza crust
- cup chowchow
- 2 cup warm barbecue sauce

Directions:

1. Spread crust evenly with chow-chow; top with pork and cheese.
2. Bake at 450° for 12 to 14 minutes or until cheese is melted.
3. Drizzle evenly with warm barbecue sauce.

Basil And Three Cheese Thin Crust Pizza

Ingredients:

Dough:

- teaspoon honey
- 1/2 teaspoons active dry yeast
- 2 cup warm water (100° to 110°)
- 1/4 cups all-purpose flour (about 5 1/2 ounces), divided
- 4 teaspoon salt
- Cooking spray
- tablespoons stone-ground yellow cornmeal
- 1/2 teaspoons olive oil

Remaining:

- Spicy Pizza Sauce

- 4 cup (3 ounces) shredded part-skim mozzarella cheese

- 2 cup part-skim ricotta

- tablespoons finely grated fresh Parmesan cheese

- tablespoons thinly sliced fresh basil

Directions:

1. To prepare dough, dissolve honey and yeast in 1/2 cup warm water in a large bowl; let stand 5 minutes. Lightly spoon flour into dry measuring cups; level with a knife. Add 1 cup flour and salt to yeast mixture; stir until a soft dough forms. Turn dough out onto a lightly floured surface. Knead until smooth and elastic (about 6 minutes); add enough of the

remaining flour, 1 tablespoon at a time, to prevent dough from sticking to hands (dough will feel slightly sticky). Place dough in a large bowl coated with cooking spray, turning to coat top. Cover and chill 1 hour.

2. Position one oven rack in the middle setting. Position another rack in the lowest setting, and place a rimless baking sheet on the bottom rack. Preheat oven to 500°.

3. Roll dough into a 13-inch circle (about 1/4 inch thick) on a lightly floured surface. Place dough on a rimless baking sheet sprinkled with cornmeal. Crimp edges of dough with fingers to form a rim. Brush oil over dough. Remove preheated baking sheet from oven; close oven door. Slide dough onto preheated baking sheet, using a spatula as a guide. Bake on lowest oven rack at 500° for 5 minutes. Remove from oven.

4. Spread Spicy Pizza Sauce in an even layer over crust, leaving a 1/4-inch border. Combine mozzarella and ricotta; sprinkle evenly over sauce.

5. Top with Parmesan. Bake on middle rack an additional 10 minutes or until crust is golden brown and cheese melts. Sprinkle with basil. Cut into 8 wedges.

Keto Pepperoni Pizza

Ingredients:

- 80 g thinly sliced pepperoni
- 100 g thinly sliced green bell pepper
- 50 g thinly sliced red onions
- freshly basil leaves, torn
- 3 tablespoons freshly grated parmesan
- 3 tablespoons extra-virgin olive oil
- cooking spray
- 2 large eggs
- 350 g grated mozzarella
- 70 g almond flour
- 170 g low-carb sugar-free tomato sauce

- 1 teaspoon crushed chilli flakes

Directions:

1. Preheat oven to 220°C (200ºC fan). Grease a baking tray with cooking spray.
2. In a food processor, pulse together eggs, 250g mozzarella, and almond flour until smooth. Spread mixture evenly in a circle on prepared sheet tray.
3. Bake until lightly golden, about ten minutes.
4. Turn crust ugly and spread pizza sauce along with baked crust.
5. Top with remaining mozzarella, pepperoni, peppers, and onions.
6. Bake until cheese is melty and crust is crisp, about a quarter-hour more.
7. Top with basil, Parmesan, essential olive oil, and chilli flakes. Slice and serve from pan while still warm.

Keto Pizza Chicken Recipe

Ingredients:

- 1 cup pizza sauces or marinara sauce ((make sure it has no added sugar))
- 2 ounces sliced pepperoni ((i like this one from applegate))
- 1 1/2 to 2 cups shredded mozzarella
- 2 tbsp avocado or olive oil
- 2 pounds boneless skinless chicken thighs
- salt and pepper

Directions:

1. Preheat oven to 350F.
2. Heat oil in a big 12-inch skillet over medium heat (be it a cast-iron skillet, be generous using your oil to avoid sticking). Sprinkle

chicken thighs with salt and pepper and to pan.
3. Cook until lightly browned, 2 to 4 minutes per side.
4. Pour pizza sauce over chicken thighs, spreading to coat.
5. Arrange pepperoni over chicken and sprinkle with mozzarella.
6. Bake 25 minutes, then start broiler for simply a short while until cheese is bubbly and browned in spots.

Gluten Free Pizza With Figs, Feta And Kale Pesto

Ingredients:

Base

- 250g buckwheat flour
- 40g tapioca flour (also called starch)
- 30g chickpea flour (gram)
- 1 Tbs psyllium husk
- Tsp salt
- 200mls warm water (40 - 45 C)
- tsp unrefined cane sugar (rapadura)
- 2 tsps dried active yeast
- 1 Tbs olive oil + extra for drizzling on base

Toppings

- 60g feta, crumbled
- A few dollops of kale & almond pesto
- 1 x quantity tomato sauce
- 4 figs, thinly sliced
- Black pepper

Directions:

1. First activate your yeast. Stir the sugar into the warm water, then sprinkle over your yeast, and leave it for 5 minutes, by which time it should be frothy. If not then your yeast is likely dead, start again.
2. Meanwhile mix your dry Ingredients:together - buckwheat, tapioca, chickpea flours, psyllium husk and salt.
3. Make a well in the middle then when the yeast is ready pour in along with the olive oil.

4. Stir clockwise with a wooden spoon bringing the Ingredients: together,
5. Finally go in with your hands and work the Ingredients: into a dough. If too dry add a tsp of water at a time, the dough should be dry, not sticky.
6. Place in a lightly oiled dough cover with a damp towel or plastic wrap and leave in a warm place for 20-30 mins. The dough will barely rise, be warned.
7. Slide your cast iron pan/bake stone into the oven and pre-heat the oven to its highest setting.
8. When the dough is proved, split into 2 and then roll out into a round pizza 0.5 cm thick by placing the dough in-between 2 sheets of parchment paper.
9. Using a rolling pin on top of the parchment to start with is helpful, but then lift off the paper

and use my your hands to tidy and manipulate the edges into a pleasing shape. If pizza looks dry and like it might crack, brush over 1/2 - 1 tsp olive oil.

10. Turn the oven down to 230C. Pick up the parchment holding the pizza and carefully slide it into the oven on top of the bakestone. Cook for 8 mins.
11. Remove the pizza on its parchment and spread half of the tomato sauce on top. Next scatter over the figs and feta and slide back into the oven for a further 5 mins or until the cheese is browned.
12. Remove the pizza from the oven, peel it from the parchment paper, slice and eat.

Sweet Italian Sausage Gluten-Free Pizza

Ingredients:

- 1 package Applegate Organic Sweet Italian Sausage, sliced
- 3 teaspoons balsamic vinegar
- 3 teaspoons chopped fresh sage
- 1/2 teaspoon freshly ground black pepper
- 1 package Applegate Natural Emmentaler Swiss Cheese
- 2 ripe pears, cored and sliced
- 3 tablespoons sesame seeds
- 1 box King Arthur Gluten Free Bread and Pizza Mix
- 4 tablespoons melted butter

- 1 3/4 cups lukewarm milk

- 3 large room temperature eggs

- 4 teaspoons olive oil (or more for pans)

- 1 large Vidalia onion, diced

Directions:

For the Crust

1. Make the pizza dough according to package Directions:, allow to rest covered in a bowl for 30 minutes.
2. Preheat the oven to 400°F. Lightly coat a large baking sheet with olive oil.
3. Stir dough to deflate, and divide the rested dough in half.
4. Drizzle dough with olive oil, and pat each into a 12 - to 14- inch round on the baking sheet.
5. Bake crusts until tops and bottoms begin to brown (about 8 to 12 minutes).

6. Remove from oven.

Pizza With Spinach, Red Onions, Mushrooms, And Pepperonis

Ingredients:

- 3/4 to 1 cup shredded vegan mozzarella-style cheese About

- 11/2 ounces fresh baby spinach About 1 cup sliced button or cremini mushrooms About

- 21/2 cups Pepperoni Crumbles about

- 1 batch pizza dough

- 1/2 cup Tomato-Garlic Pizza Sauce

- 1/3 red onion, thinly sliced

Directions:

1. While you are making the pizza, put a pizza stone in the oven and heat it to 500 degrees Fahrenheit for 30 minutes.
2. The dough should be cut in half so that the pieces are of equal size.
3. Keep one and put the other back in the bucket, covered, in the fridge for later.
4. You can either make one big circle or two smaller ones, by stretching or rolling out the dough on a lightly floured surface until it is as thin as you can get it.
5. My personal preference is to make little pizzas around 11 inches in diameter and large pizzas approximately 14 or 15 inches.
6. You shouldn't stress if your dough tears. Simply use your fingertips to make a temporary repair.
7. If the dough is too sticky, sprinkle it lightly with flour.

8. Overusing it will result in a dry crust. Roll out the dough, then carefully move it to a large piece of parchment paper.
9. Spread the tomato sauce (about 1/4 cup for each small pizza, and about 1/2 cup for a large) evenly on the pizza, leaving a 1/4- to 1/2-inch border around the edge.
10. Sprinkle the cheese over the sauce, and top with an even layer of the spinach and mushrooms.
11. Sprinkle an even layer of the Pepperoni Crumbles on top of the mushrooms and top with the onion slices. If making 2 small pizzas, repeat with the remaining pizza.
12. When using a pizza stone, carefully move the pizza and parchment paper to the stone.
13. If you don't have a pizza stone, just bake the pizza directly on a baking sheet in a hot oven. The second pizza should be made in the same

manner if you want to make two individual pizzas.

14. Leave it in the oven for 10–15 minutes, or until the crust is very dark brown and the cheese is melted.
15. If it is not yet done, bake it for a few more minutes.
16. Hold off on serving the pizza for 5 minutes after it's finished baking.

Pizza With Green Olives And Basil

Ingredients:

- 1 batch pizza dough
- 1/2 cup Tomato-Garlic Pizza Sauce
- 1 cup shredded vegan mozzarella-style cheese
- 1-ounce fresh whole basil leaves,

Directions:

1. While you are preparing the pizza, preheat the oven to 500 degrees Fahrenheit for 30 minutes with a pizza stone inside.
2. Cut the dough in half so that each half is about the same size.
3. Reserve 1 for use and put the other back into the bucket with a lid and into the fridge.
4. On a lightly floured surface, stretch or roll out your dough into 1 large or 2 small rounds. The

pizzas of my choice have a diameter of 11 inches for the small size and 14–15 inches for the large.
5. If your dough breaks, that's okay. Just use your fingertips to make a quick repair.
6. If the dough is too sticky, dust a little more flour on it.
7. Overusing it will result in a dry crust. Move the rolled-out dough on a large piece of parchment paper with care.
8. Spread the tomato sauce (about 1/4 cup for each small pizza, and about 1/2 cup for a large) evenly on the pizza, leaving a 1/4- to 1/2-inch border around the edge. Sprinkle the cheese over the sauce.
9. If making 2 small pizzas, repeat with the remaining pizza.
10. With care, transport the pizza and parchment paper (if used) to the pizza stone. If you don't

have a pizza stone, just bake the pizza directly on a baking sheet in a hot oven.
11. The second pizza should be made in the same manner if you want to make two individual pizzas.
12. Put it in the oven for 10 to 15 minutes, or until the crust is a nice, deep brown and the cheese is melted. Bake for a few more minutes if necessary.
13. The pizza needs to rest for 5 minutes. Before slicing, sprinkle the basil strips on top and serve immediately.

Creamy Salmon Shirataki Fettucine

Ingredients:

For the shirataki fettuccine:

- 2 (8 oz) packs shirataki fettuccine

For the creamy salmon sauce:

- 1 ¼ cups heavy cream

- ½ cup dry white wine

- 1 tsp grated lemon zest

- 1 cup baby spinach

- Lemon wedges for garnishing

- 5 tbsp butter

- 4 salmon fillets, cut into 2-inch cubes

- Salt and black pepper to taste

- 3 garlic cloves, minced

Directions:

For the shirataki fettuccine:

1. Boil 2 cups of water in a pot over medium heat.
2. Strain the shirataki pasta through a colander and rinse very well under hot running water.
3. Pour the shirataki pasta into the boiling water. Take off the heat, let sit for 3 minutes and strain again.
4. Place a dry skillet over medium heat and stir-fry the shirataki pasta until visibly dry, and makes a squeaky sound when stirred, 1 to 2 minutes. Take off the heat and set aside.
5. For the salmon sauce:
6. Melt half of the butter in a large skillet; season the salmon with salt, black pepper, and cook in the butter until golden brown on

all sides and flaky within, 8 minutes. Transfer to a plate and set aside.

7. Add the remaining butter to the skillet to melt and stir in the garlic. Cook until fragrant, 1 minute.
8. Mix in heavy cream, white wine, lemon zest, salt, and pepper.
9. Allow boiling over low heat for 5 minutes.
10. Stir in spinach, allow wilting for 2 minutes and stir in shirataki fettuccine and salmon until well-coated in the sauce. Garnish with the lemon wedges.

Creamy Mussel With Shirataki

Ingredients:

For the angel hair shirataki:

- 2 (8 oz) packs angel hair shirataki

For the creamy mussels:

- 6 garlic cloves, minced

- 2 tsp red chili flakes

- ½ cup fish stock

- 1 ½ cups heavy cream

- 2 tbsp chopped fresh parsley

- 1 lb mussels, debearded and rinsed

- 1 cup white wine

- 4 tbsp olive oil

- 3 shallots, finely chopped

- Salt and black pepper to taste

Directions:

For the angel hair shirataki:

1. Bring 2 cups of water to a boil in a pot over medium heat.
2. Strain shirataki pasta through a colander and rinse very well under hot running water. Remove pot from the heat.
3. Drain and transfer the shirataki into boiling water.
4. Take off the heat, let sit for 3 minutes and strain again.
5. Place a large dry skillet over medium heat and stir-fry the shirataki pasta until visibly dry, 1 to 2 minutes. Take off the heat and set aside.
6. For the creamy mussels:
7. Pour mussels and white wine into a pot, cover, and cook for 4 minutes.

8. Occasionally stir until the mussels have opened. Strain the mussels and reserve the cooking liquid.
9. Allow cooling, discard any mussels with closed shells, and remove the meat out of ¾ of the mussel shells.
10. Set aside with the remaining mussels in the shells.
11. Heat olive oil in a skillet and sauté shallots, garlic, and chili flakes for 3 minutes. Mix in reduced wine and fish stock.
12. Allow boiling and whisk in the remaining butter and then the heavy cream.
13. Taste the sauce and adjust the taste with salt, pepper, and mix in parsley.
14. Pour in the shirataki pasta, mussels and toss well in the sauce. Serve afterwards.

Garbanzo-Onion Bread

Ingredients:

- 1 teaspoon xanthan gum

- 4 eggs (200 g)

- 1 cup (230 g) low-sodium chicken broth or vegetable broth

- 1 cup (230 g) water

- ½ cup (120 g) salted butter or margarine, melted

- ½ cup (100 g) chopped fresh onion

- 2 cups (230 g) garbanzo bean flour

- 1 cup (120 g) almond flour

- 4 teaspoons baking powder

- ¼ cup Splenda or Stevia Extract

- Salt

Directions:

1. Warm up the oven to 3700F.
2. Grease the baking tray with oil and you can as well line the base of the pan with a parchment paper. .
3. In a mixing bowl, pour in the dry ingredients which includes garbanzo flour, almond flour, xanthan gum, sweetener, baking powder and combine thoroughly.
4. In a separate container, or preferable an electric mixer, mix the milk, water, eggs, butter till a thorough formulation is achieved. Sprinkle in the onion in generous quantity.
5. Combine the dry and wet mixture with the mixer for about 5 minutes till a tacky dough is formed.

6. Transfer the flour mix into the greased baking tray.
7. Bake for about 35 minutes, turn the other side of the dough and bake for another 35 minutes till a toothpick or knife comes out lean from the centre of the loaf.
8. Allow the bread to cool down a little in the pan for about 10 minutes just before you turn out the loaf.
9. Allow the loaf to cool on the wire rack for about 15 minutes before portioning into smaller quantities.

Onion And Poppy Seed Bread

Ingredients:

- 2 teaspoons poppy seeds

- 1 teaspoon xanthan gum

- 4 eggs (200 g)

- 1 cup (230 g) unsweetened soy milk or other milk

- ½ cup (120g) butter or margarine

- ½ cup (80 g) chopped fresh onion

- Salt (as desired)

- 1 ½ cups (180 g) golden flaxseed meal

- 1 ½ cups (180 g) sesame seed flour

- Splenda or Stevia Extract in the Raw

- 4 teaspoons baking powder

Directions:

1. Warm up the oven to 3700F. Grease the baking tray with oil and you can as well line the base of the pan with a parchment paper.
2. In a mixing bowl, pour in the dry ingredients which includes sesame flour, poppy seeds, flaxseed meal xanthan gum, sweetener, baking powder and combine thoroughly.
3. In a separate container, or preferable an electric mixer, mix the milk, water, eggs, butter till a thorough formulation is achieved.
4. Sprinkle in the onion in generous quantity.
5. Combine the dry and wet mixture with the mixer for about 5 minutes till a tacky dough is formed.
6. Transfer the flour mix into the greased baking tray.
7. Bake for about 35 minutes, turn the other side of the dough and bake for another 35 minutes

till a toothpick or knife comes out lean from the centre of the loaf.
8. Allow the bread to cool down a little in the pan for about 10 minutes just before you turn out the loaf.
9. Allow the loaf to cool on the wire rack for about 15 minutes before portioning into smaller quantities.
10. Hazelnut Bread
11. As the name implies, the hazelnut is the secret behind the flour-rich taste of this Ingredients: and it can be used in making a variety of sandwiches.

School Pizza

Ingredients:

Dough:

- 2 tbsp. yogurt
- 1/2 tsp soda
- 1/4 tsp salt
- 50 g cold margarine or butter
- 100 g flour

Filling:

- 2 tbsp. tomato paste or ketchup
- Grated cheese
- Sliced sausage, ham or sausage

- Finely chopped onion, olives, parsley (optional)

Directions:

1. Margarine grate, add flour, yogurt, baking soda, and salt. All mix, knead the dough.
2. Roll out the dough thinly on a baking sheet, greased or oiled.
3. Coat it with two tablespoons of tomato paste or ketchup. Sprinkle with cheese. On the cheese to put diced ham or cooked sausage, mix with finely chopped onions.
4. Put in a preheated 180° C oven and bake for about 15 minutes. Pizza is ready.

Closed Pizza

Ingredients:

For the dough:

- 2.5 cups flour
- Salt
- 2 tbsp. vegetable oil
- 1 tsp dry yeast
- 2/3 cup of warm milk
- 1 tbsp. Sahara

For filling:

- 600 g minced
- Salt pepper
- 1 tomato

- 1/3 cup olive

- Mayonnaise, ketchup

- 200 g of cheese

- Poppy seeds or sesame seeds for sprinkling

- 1 egg

- 2 onions

- Vegetable oil for frying

- 1 sweet pepper

Directions:

1. Yeast breed in warm milk, add sugar, let stand for 10 minutes, the yeast began to react.
2. Gradually add the sifted flour and butter. Knead the dough.
3. Leave for 1 hour in a warm place for the dough approached.

4. Prepare the filling: finely chop the onion and fry it until transparent in vegetable oil, add the peppers, cut into strips.
5. Separately, fry the beef until cooked, add salt, pepper and chopped tomato.
6. When the dough is suitable to cut it into two parts.
7. From each roll out a rectangle. Lubricate each layer of mayonnaise and ketchup.
8. Put the onion and pepper, then mince, olives.
9. Sprinkle with cheese. Scrapie edge, put on a baking sheet seam down.
10. Coat lightly with beaten egg and sprinkle with poppy seeds. Give 15-20 minutes to go.
11. Then put in the oven. Bake for 20-30 minutes at 180 C, until golden brown.
12. Ready-made cakes remove from oven, let stand 10 minutes, then can be cut.

Best-Ever Homemade Pizza

Ingredients:

- 3 cups all-purpose flour

- 2 teaspoons kosher salt

- 1/4 cup extra-virgin olive oil

- Extra-virgin olive oil , as needed

- 1/4 cup cornmeal , divided

- 1 cup marinara, divided

- 16 ounces fresh mozzarella, thinly sliced, divided

- Fresh basil leaves

- Pinch red pepper flakes

- Cooking spray

- 1 1/4 cups . Lukewarm water

- 1 tablespoon granulated sugar

- 1 1/4 packets 1 (1/4-oz.) Active dry yeast (2 1/4 tsp.)

Directions:

1. Excess fat a sizable pan combined with cooking aerosol.
2. Within a tiny pan put water in addition to glucose and blend to dissolve, and then mix over fungus enabling sit right up until creamy, about 7 mins. In one more huge bowl, put flour, salt, in addition to olive oil.
3. Are harvested yeast blend, and then mix together together with a wooden location until everything is normally combined and furthermore a shaggy money commences to become able to type.

4. Knead in resistance to sides associated with pan until money commences ahead together, and then turn onto your current work surface in addition to knead, adding a new pinch of flour if needed, right up until it feels stretchy and only a little tacky, 5 mins.

5. Form in to a restricted ball, place directly into prepared bowl, in addition to cover utilizing a clear dish towel.

6. Permit rise in a new warm spot inside your kitchen until bending in size, concerning one hour and thirty minutes.

7. Gently strike down dough, after that divide in two, and roll in to balls.

8. At this time, a person can freeze 1, or make 2 pizzas.

9. Let money balls rest while you preheat oven in order to 500° and oil a huge baking page with olive essential oil.

10. Sprinkle throughout along with 2 tablespoons cornmeal.
11. On your function surface, gently trim one ball associated with dough and move with a moving pin (or extend together with your hands) till about 12" within diameter (as slim while you can).
12. Cautiously transfer to ready sheet pan and clean dough all more than with oil.
13. After that, add your 0. 5 cup sauce in order to middle of money and spread outwards with a tea spoon or ladle, leaving behind about 1" for that crust.
14. Top along with half the pieces of mozzarella. Cook until crust will be golden and parmesan cheese is melty, regarding a quarter-hour.
15. Top along with fresh basil simply leaves, a drizzle associated with olive oil, plus red pepper flakes.

16. Repeat with leftover dough and toppings for second pizzas.

Blackberry Ricotta Pizza With Basil

Ingredients:

- 1 cup swiss cheese swiss cheese or mozzarella shredded

- 3/4 cup ricotta

- 1/2 cup blackberries blackberries whole

- 1/4 cup green onion green onions chopped

- 1/2 teaspoon salt salt more to taste

- Pepper ground pepper to taste (i like lots)

- 2 tablespoons basil fresh basil chopped

- One pizza dough recipe (to make one 12-inch pizza)*

- 1 tablespoon olive oil olive oil

- 1/2 cup blackberries fresh blackberries smashed

- 1 cup parmesan shredded

Directions:

1. Preheat your oven to 450 degrees F.
2. Put your pizza stone in the oven if you have one.
3. Roll out your pizza dough on a floured sheet of parchment paper to about 12 inches. (If you don't have a pizza stone, you should probably transfer the dough to a baking sheet now.)

4. Drizzle 1 tablespoon of olive oil over the top of the dough and use your fingers or a pastry brush to coat well, especially the edges. Use a fork to mash a half cup of blackberries in a bowl. It doesn't have got to be best.
5. Utilize the fork or perhaps a slotted place to ladle typically the pulp onto typically the pizza.
6. Spread that around the same way you would french fries sauce. (You may need the staying juice, but may throw it out there.
7. Drink that nice nectar if an individual know what's useful to you.) Top typically the smashed berries together with 1 cup Parmesan and 1 glass swiss or mozzarella, making sure to find the crust. Use a new spoon to scrap the ricotta above the pizza.
8. That doesn't have to be able to be perfect. Leading with whole refreshing blackberries and sliced green onions.

9. Add salt, and put pepper to preference. If the oven is usually hot, transfer typically the pizza to typically the oven.
10. I exchange it employing a a new flat baking linen, still on typically the parchment paper.
11. Make for about 8-10 minutes, or before the top has started out to brown.
12. An individual can broil that for a second if you wish it crispier on top.
13. Get rid of through the oven in addition to immediately sprinkle several chopped basil about top. Slice in addition to enjoy!

Pizza Bianca

Ingredients:

- 12 ounces mozzarella cheese, shredded
- 2 teaspoons chopped rosemary (or basil)
- 1/8 teaspoon salt
- 1 pizza dough (12-inch size)
- 1/2 cup chopped white onion

Directions:

1. Preheat the oven to 450 degrees. Stretch the dough into a 12-inch pizza pan and sprinkle the dough with the salt.
2. Sprinkle the onion and cheese over the crust, distributing it evenly.
3. Top the cheese with the rosemary.

4. Bake for 10-20 minutes or until the crust is done and the cheese is melted.

Bbq Chicken Pizza

Ingredients:

- 2 prepared and cooked pizza crusts (about 8-inches each)
- 1/2 purple onion, sliced
- 1/4 cup each: soft cream cheese and diced green chilies
- 1/2 cup jack cheese, shredded
- 1/4 teaspoon hot pepper flakes, or to taste
- 1 pound cooked chicken
- 1/3 cup BBQ sauce (any flavor)
- Salt and pepper to taste
- 4 ounces bacon in 1-inch pieces, cooked and drained

Directions:

1. Combine the chicken and the BBQ sauce; mix well and set aside for 5 minutes.
2. Spread each crust with 2 tablespoons cream cheese; divide the chicken in the sauce evenly between the two pizzas.
3. Top each with equal amounts of the remaining Ingredients:, including the bacon. Set aside while the oven preheats.
4. Preheat the oven to 400 degrees.
5. Bake the pizzas for 15-20 minutes each or until the cheese is melted and slightly browned.

Pizza On The Grill Pan

Ingredients:

- 150 g hard cheese
- 2-3 tbsp ketchup
- 4-5 fresh champignon
- Frozen pizza dough
- 2 fresh tomatoes
- 100 g smoked sausage

Directions:
1. For a start cut products for pizza. Cut tomatoes into thin slices.
2. Cut the mushrooms into slices. Sausage can take any, you can replace it with ham. Cut the sausage into thin slices.
3. Rub the cheese on a large grater.

4. Now the dough. Suitable conventional yeast dough on the water.
5. Roll out the dough very thin (3-4 mm). Send the dough into the pan. A few spoons of ketchup for the taste.
6. Spread the ketchup well. The sausage sent to the dough. Now make a layer of tomatoes. and mushrooms are sent to the pan.
7. And now the cheese, which is sent to the pan.
8. Send the pan on a small fire and cover it with a lid.
9. Cook pizza for 15-20 minutes. The finished pizza still warm serve.

Pizza Margarita In The Grill

Ingredients:

- Olive oil 20 ml

- Salt 1/4 tsp

- Sauce tomatoes in own juice 200 grams

- Garlic 1 clove

- Herbs de Provence 1/2 tsp

- Active dry yeast 2 grams

- Baking flour 320 grams

- Water 160 ml

- Salt and sugar to taste

Directions:

1. Prepare the dough for the pizza. Yeast is soluble in warm water.
2. Add half of the olive oil and flour and knead the dough. In the process, add the remaining oil and salt.
3. Mash until smooth. Divide the dough into 3 parts, from each form a ball. Put each in a separate floured bowl, cover with film and refrigerate overnight. Prepare the tomato sauce.
4. Knead the tomatoes and put in a saucepan with the juice.
5. Add the herbs, bring to a boil and cook over medium heat for 5 minutes.
6. Add finely chopped garlic, salt and sugar to taste, heat for 1 minute.
7. Remove from heat and interrupt the blender.
8. Three mozzarella on a coarse grater. Proceed to baking pizza. Kindle the grill. Put it in the convector.

9. Placed on Converter a pizza stone. Cover and heat the grill to 200 degrees. Roll out dough.
10. Grease with tomato sauce.
11. Put the mozzarella on the sauce. Put the pizza on the hot stone. Bake with the lid closed for about 5 minutes until the cheese melts.

Eggplant Parmesan Slices

Ingredients:

- 1 cup Parmesan Cheese
- Sauce, Cheese and Toppings of choice
- 1 Eggplant
- 2 Eggs + 1 tbsp Water
- 1 cup Almond Flour

Directions:

1. Slice the eggplant lengthwise (multiple slices).
2. Dip the slices in almond flour, then in an egg mixture and lastly in parmesan cheese.
3. Line eggplant on parchment lined sheet pan.
4. Bake on 350F for 15 min or until golden brown.

5. Take out the oven, cool for 5 minutes then top slices with sauce, cheese and toppings.
6. Bake for 10 minutes or until cheese is melted.
7. Let cool slightly before eating. Enjoy!

Rosemary, Feta Cheese And Dried Tomato

Ingredients:

- 1/4 teaspoon fresh garlic, minced

- 150 g (1 1/2 cups) feta cheese, crumbled

- 120 ml (1/2 cup) cold pressed, extra virgin olive oil

- 250 ml (2 cups) buttermilk

- 1 egg, beaten

- Sea salt, to taste

- 250 g (2 cups) your choice flour

- 2 teaspoons baking powder

- 80 g (about 3 ounces) sun-dried tomatoes, finely chopped

- 2 sprigs fresrosemary, finely chopped

Directions:

1. Preheat oven to 220 degrees Celsius (425 degrees Fahrenheit)
2. Roll out the pastry as per Directions: and prepare crust. Pre-bake in oven for about 15 minutes.
3. In a large bowl, combine flour and baking powder.
4. Add in sun-dried tomatoes, rosemary, garlic and feta. Stir just to combine.
5. In a second, small bowl whisk together egg, oil and buttermilk.
6. With the bottom of a cup or the back of a spoon, dig a small bowl into the dry Ingredients:.
7. Pour the wet Ingredients: into the dry, and mix just until combined. (Don't over mix or your muffins will be heavy.) You want the dough to be a little lumpy – even showing dry

Ingredients: still is good. The batter will be thick.

8. Carefully spoon batter into mini-muffin cups, wiping off any spills. (It happens.)
9. Place on middle rack in oven and bake for 12 – 15 minutes. Muffins are done when toothpick inserted into center comes out clean.

French Riviera Savory Herb And Bourse Mini-Muffins

Ingredients:

- 1 large egg

- 150g Boursin cheese (fine herbs or garlic herbs) at room temperature, stirred until creamy

- 180ml (3/4 cup) milk

- 2 teaspoons fresh chives, finely chopped

- 200g (1 cup) flour of your choice

- 50g (1/4 cup) oat bran

- 1 level tablespoon baking powder

- 1/2 teaspoon salt

- 1/4 teaspoon freshly ground black pepper

Directions:

1. Preheat oven to 180 degrees Celsius (350 degrees Fahrenheit)
2. Preheat the oven to 180 C / Gas 4. Line a muffin tray with paper cases.
3. In a large bowl, mix the flour, oat bran, baking powder, salt and pepper. Make a well out of the dry mixture.
4. Mix the egg with the milk and Boursin and mix well (it should not form lumps, if it does, the Boursin is too cold).
5. Fold wet mixture into the flour mixture and stir just until mixed. It's okay if it has lumps.
6. Carefully spoon the mixture into the muffin cases and wipe away any drips.
7. bake for 10 – 13 minutes in the preheated oven, until a toothpick inserted into a muffin cup comes out clean.
8. Let cool for 5 minutes, then un-mold, an let cool on wire rack.

Marguerite Pizza

Ingredients:

- 1 tablespoon olive oil

- 2 cloves garlic, finely chopped

- 1/4 cup pizza sauce

- 8 oz. mozzarella cheese

- 2 tomatoes, sliced

- fresh basil

- fresh ground pepper, to taste

Directions:

1. Combine the olive oil and chopped garlic in a small dish.
2. Cook cream cheese keto crust as stated above.

3. Remove crust from the oven and increase oven temperature to 450°F.
4. Spread baked keto crust with olive oil/garlic mixture.
5. Top with pizza sauce, mozzarella cheese slices, and tomato slices.
6. Bake until cheese is melted. Remove from the oven. Top with basil and pepper before serving.

Marinara Pizza

Ingredients:

- 1 1/2 cup mozzarella cheese, grated
- 100 g cherry tomatoes, halved
- 1/2 cup cooked salmon, chopped
- 1 ounce sliced black olives, drained
- 1 teaspoon dried oregano
- 2 tablespoons olive oil
- 3 cloves garlic, finely chopped
- 1/3 cup your favorite pizza sauce
- Handful of fresh basil

Directions:

1. Mix olive oil and chopped garlic in a small dish.
2. Cook cream cheese keto crust as stated above.
3. Remove crust from the oven and increase oven temperature to 450°F.
4. Spread baked keto crust with olive oil/garlic mixture.
5. Spread tomato sauce, dried oregano, cherry tomatoes, salmon, and sliced black olives.
6. Top with mozzarella cheese and fresh basil.
7. Bake for 5 to 10 minutes until cheese is melted. Serve and enjoy!

Blackberry Brie Pizzettas

Ingredients:

- tablespoons extra virgin olive oil, divided
- ounces Brie cheese, trimmed and sliced*
- 1/2 cups fresh blackberries, halved
- 4 cup chopped toasted pecans
- cups loosely packed fresh arugula
- 4 cup torn basil leaves
- tablespoons butter
- large sweet onion, thinly sliced
- medium-size fennel bulb, thinly sliced (optional)
- Pizzetta Dough*

- Parchment paper

- teaspoons balsamic vinegar

Directions:

1. Preheat oven to 425°. Melt butter in a large skillet over medium-high heat; add onion and, if desired, fennel, and cook, stirring often, 20 minutes or until golden brown.
2. Flour hands, and shape each Peseta Dough ball into a 6- to 8-inch round. Place each round on a small piece of parchment paper.
3. Brush with 1 Tbsp. oil. Top dough rounds with cheese, next 2 Ingredients:, and onion mixture.
4. Place 4 pizzettas (on parchment paper) directly on oven rack, and bake at 425° for 12 to 14 minutes or until golden. Repeat with remaining dough rounds.

5. Toss together arugula, next 2 Ingredients:, and remaining 1 Tbsp. oil. Add salt and pepper to taste.
6. Sprinkle baked pizzettas with arugula mixture just before serving.
7. *1 lb. store-bought pizza dough and 8 oz. sliced or shredded mozzarella cheese may be substituted.

Breakfast Pizza

Ingredients:

- Cup frozen shredded hash brown potatoes, thawed
- Cup (4 ounces) shredded fat-free cheddar cheese
- 4 cup fat-free milk
- 2 teaspoon salt
- 8 teaspoon black pepper
- (8-ounce) carton egg substitute
- (8-ounce) can reduced-fat refrigerated crescent dinner roll dough
- Cooking spray
- Ounces turkey breakfast sausage

- Tablespoons grated fresh parmesan cheese

Directions:

1. Preheat oven to 375°.
2. Separate dough into triangles. Press triangles together to form a single round crust on a 12-inch pizza pan coated with cooking spray.
3. Crimp edges of dough with fingers to form a rim.
4. Cook sausage in a large nonstick skillet over medium heat until browned, stirring to crumble. Drain.
5. Top prepared dough with sausage, potatoes, and cheese.
6. Combine milk, salt, pepper, and egg substitute, stirring with a whisk.
7. Carefully pour milk mixture over sausage mixture. Sprinkle with Parmesan.
8. Bake at 375° for 25 minutes or until crust is browned.

Keto Pizza Chicken

Ingredients:

- 1 egg
- 1 tablespoon heavy whipping cream
- 2 large chicken breasts, sliced in half
- 1 1/2 cups tomato sauce (such as rao's®)
- 16 slices pepperoni
- 2 cups shredded mozzarella cheese
- 1 (16-ounce) package pork rinds, crushed
- 2 tablespoons chopped fresh parsley
- 1 tablespoon garlic powder
- 1 tablespoon paprika
- 4 tablespoons avocado oils

Directions:

1. Combine pork rinds, parsley, garlic powder, and paprika in a resealable plastic bag. Mix well and reserve. Advertisement
2. Heat oil in a cast iron skillet over medium heat.
3. Mix egg and cream together in a bowl to produce a wash.
4. Dip 1 little bit of chicken in to the wash and drop in to the bag of pork rinds. Shake to coat completely and transfer to a plate. Repeat with remaining chicken. Put coated chicken in to the hot oil in the skillet and cook until crispy no longer pink inside, three to four 4 minutes per side.
5. Remove skillet from heat and top each little bit of chicken with 1/3 cup tomato sauce. Add 4 slices of pepperoni to each chicken and cover with mozzarella cheese.

6. Set an oven rack about 6 inches from heat source and preheat the oven's broiler.
7. Broil chicken in the preheated oven until cheese is melted and slightly browned, about five minutes.

Keto Pizza Crust - Plain Chicken

Ingredients:

- 1/2 teaspoon dried oregano

- 3 tablespoons coconut oils

- 1 egg, lightly beaten

- 2/3 cup almond flour (5.25-oz)

- 1/2 teaspoon salt

- 1/2 cup finely grated Parmesan cheese

Directions:

1. Preheat oven to 350ºF. Combine almond flour, salt, parmesan cheese, and oregano in a bowl.
2. Whisk together coconut oil and egg. Make a well in the heart of the dry Ingredients: and add the egg mixture.

3. Stir well before mixture all fits in place in a ball. Roll the dough out to a 12-inch circle in-between two sheets of parchment paper.
4. Put on a pizza stone or baking tray. Take away the top sheet of parchment paper. Bake 8 - ten minutes.
5. Remove from the oven. Top partially baked crust with sauce and desired toppings.
6. Go back to oven and bake yet another 8 to ten minutes. Allow pizza to cool five minutes before slicing.

Three Cheese Pizza

Ingredients:

Pizza Crust

- 3/4 to 1 cup warm water

- 1 packet nutritional yeast

- 2 teaspoons sea salt & pepper

- dried herbs of your choosing (basil, oregano, rosemary and thyme)

- 2 1/4 cups all purpose flour

- 1/2 teaspoon sugar

- 2 tablespoons olive oil

Sauce

- handful fresh basil leaves

- 1/2 teaspoon chili flakes
- 2-5 garlic cloves
- 3 tablespoons sun-dried tomatoes
- 1 1/2 tablespoons agave
- water as needed
- 1 tablespoon olive oil (or use pine nuts and water)
- 1 tablespoon tamari
- 1 tablespoon rice wine vinegar (or apple cider vinegar)
- 2 tablespoons mustard
- a few drops of liquid smoke

Toppings

- Grilled eggplant slices

- 1 cup cooked black rice mix

- Handful basil leaves

- 1/3 cup shredded vegan cheddar cheese

- 1/3 vegan mozzarella shredded cheese

- Pepper and/or fave dried herb mixes

- Fave hot sauce

- 2 grilled bell peppers

- Vegan parmesan

Directions:

1. Combine the yeast and warm water in a warm mixing bowl.
2. Sprinkle on a tiny bit of sugar to feed the yeast. let it rise for about 10 minutes.
3. Add the other Ingredients: and knead the dough or mix in your mixer until it's soft and

elastic; 8-10 minutes. let it rise for an hour or until it doubles in size.

4. Then roll it out into a pizza crust! partially bake it for 8-10 minutes at 425 degrees.

Quinoa Pizza Crust

Ingredients:

- 3/4 tsp. salt

- 2 clove garlic, sliced

- 1 TB. Italian seasoning

- 1 TB. nutritional yeast

- 1 cup quinoa, soaked for at least 8 hours, rinsed and drained

- 1/4-1/2 cup water

- 2 TB. coconut oil

Directions:

1. Soak the quinoa in filtered water for at least 8 hours.

2. Rinse and drain the quinoa. (If you plan this for dinner, just soak the quinoa in the morning before leaving for work or soak it overnight, rinse, drain in a.m. and put into a sealed container and keep in fridge till you get ready to make.) *This step is crucial as the recipe won't work with dry quinoa.
3. Add all of the Ingredients: to a food processor or a high-speed blender and combine until the dough resembles pancake batter. Adjust the water as needed.
4. Preheat your oven to 450 degrees and coat either a cast iron skillet or an 8-inch round cake pan (I used a cast iron skillet) with 3 TB. coconut oil.
5. Allow the skillet or cake pan to heat up in the oven for about 10 minutes (this is good to do while you're preparing the dough and chopping the veggies). Remove skillet/cake pan from the oven and immediately add the

quinoa "dough," using a spatula to even it out as needed.
6. Place the dough in the oven to bake for 20 minutes.
7. Flip the dough and bake for another 10 minutes, or until brown and crispy.
8. Add whatever toppings you want and feel free to be creative.
9. Place the pizza in the oven under the broiler after adding the toppings just to heat everything up a bit. (About 5 – 8 minutes).
10. When pizza comes out, top with fresh basil leaves, Serve.

Grilled Onion And Cheese Pizza

Ingredients:

- 1 cup shredded vegan Cheddar-or mozzarella-style cheese

- 6 small red potatoes, or more as needed, cut into paper-thin slices

- 1 batch pizza dough

- 2/3 cup Cheddar Cashew Cheese Sauce

- Thinly sliced scallions, for garnish

Directions:

1. While you are making the pizza, put a pizza stone in the oven and heat it to 500 degrees Fahrenheit for 30 minutes.
2. Cut the dough in half so you have two equal pieces. Save one for yourself, and put the

other back in the bucket, covered, in the fridge.

3. Stretch or roll out your dough on a lightly floured surface into 1 or 2 big or little rounds, as thin as you can make them.
4. The medium pizzas should be around 13 inches in diameter, the large ones at 14 or 15 inches, and mine are usually 11 inches in diameter for the small ones.
5. If your dough tears, that's okay. Simply use your fingers to make a quick repair. If the dough is too sticky, sprinkle it lightly with flour.
6. A dry crust will result from using too much.
7. Gently lift the rolled dough onto the parchment paper.
8. Spread the cheese sauce (about 1/3 cup for each small pizza, and about 2/3 cup for a large) evenly on the pizza, leaving a 1/4- to 1/2-inch border around the edge.

9. Sprinkle the cheese over the sauce, and top with an even layer of the potatoes, just slightly overlapping in a concentric circle (see tip on page 61). If making 2 small pizzas, repeat with the remaining pizza.
10. With care, move the pizza and parchment paper to the pizza stone.
11. Put the pizza on a baking sheet and bake it in the oven. Repeat with the second pizza if you want to make two individual pizzas.
12. Put it in the oven for 10 to 15 minutes to get a crust that's reasonably dark brown and the cheese melted.
13. If it isn't done after 20 minutes, keep baking it.
14. For the next 5 minutes, pizza cooling is required.
15. After the pizza has cooled, sprinkle the scallions on top and serve it in bite-sized pieces.

Beef-Asparagus Shirataki Mix

Ingredients:

For the angel hair shirataki:

- 2 (8 oz) packs angel hair shirataki

For the beef-asparagus base:

- 3 garlic cloves, minced
- Salt and black pepper to taste
- 1 cup finely grated Parmesan cheese for topping
- 1 lb ground beef
- 3 tbsp olive oil
- 1 lb fresh asparagus, cut into 1-inch pieces
- 2 large shallots, finely chopped

Directions:

For the angel hair shirataki:

1. Bring 2 cups of water to a boil in a medium pot over medium heat. Strain the shirataki pasta through a colander and rinse very well under hot running water. Drain properly and transfer the shirataki pasta into the boiling water. Cook for 3 minutes and strain again.
2. Place a dry large skillet over medium heat and stir-fry the shirataki pasta until visibly dry, 1 to 2 minutes. Take off the heat and set aside.
3. For the beef-asparagus base:
4. Heat a large non-stick skillet over medium heat and add the beef. Cook while breaking the lumps that form until brown, 10 minutes. Use a slotted spoon to transfer the beef to a plate and discard the drippings.
5. Heat olive oil in skillet and sauté asparagus until tender, 7 minutes. Stir in shallots and garlic and cook for 2 minutes. Season with salt

and pepper. Stir in the beef, shirataki and toss until well combined. Adjust the taste with salt and black pepper as desired.
6. Dish the food onto serving plates and garnish generously with the Parmesan cheese.

Garlic-Butter Steak Bites With Shirataki Fettucine

Ingredients:

For the shirataki fettuccine:

- 2 (8 oz) packs shirataki fettuccine

For the garlic-butter steak bites:

- 4 garlic cloves, mined
- 2 tbsp chopped fresh parsley
- 1 cup freshly grated Pecorino Romano cheese
- 4 tbsp butter
- 1 lb thick-cut New York strip steaks, cut into 1-inch cubes
- Salt and black pepper to taste

Directions:

For the shirataki fettuccine:

1. Boil 2 cups of water in a medium pot over medium heat.
2. Strain the shirataki pasta through a colander and rinse very well under hot running water.
3. Allow proper draining and pour the shirataki pasta into the boiling water. Cook for 3 minutes and strain again.
4. Place a dry skillet over medium heat and stir-fry the shirataki pasta until visibly dry, and makes a squeaky sound when stirred, 1 to 2 minutes. Take off the heat and set aside.
5. For the garlic-butter steak bites:
6. Melt the butter in a large skillet, season the steaks with salt, black pepper and cook in the butter until brown, and cooked through, 10 minutes.
7. Stir in the garlic and cook until fragrant, 1 minute.

8. Mix in the parsley and shirataki pasta; toss well and season with salt and black pepper.
9. Dish the food, top with the Pecorino Romano cheese and serve immediately.

Pizza From Puff Pastry With Lecho

Ingredients:

- 150 g of cheese
- 7 eggs
- Lecho any home
- for the sauce: ketchup, mayonnaise
- 250 g puff pastry
- 500 g lactic sausage
- Flour for rolling out dough

Directions:

1. The oven is heated to 220 C. Prepare the dough.
2. Roll out the dough and put it on a baking sheet and add the sauce.

3. Cut sausage into cubes.
4. Eggs cook.
5. Grate eggs on a coarse grater.
6. Cheese also grate. Put the sausage.
7. Then the eggs. Add any lecho.
8. Sprinkle with cheese and remove it in the oven.
9. After 25-30 minutes to get ready-made pizza.

Fruit Pizza

Ingredients:

- 1 1/4 cups flour

- 1 tsp baking powder

- 1/4 tsp salt

- 200 g of cream cheese (Philadelphia type)

- 1/2 cup sugar

- 2 tsp vanilla extract or vanilla sugar sachet

- 100 g butter, room temperature

- 3/4 cup sugar

- 1 egg

- Fruit

Directions:

1. Heat oven to 180 C.
2. Beat in a large bowl, cream the softened butter and 3/4 cup sugar, beating for about 5 minutes.
3. Add the egg, then the flour, baking powder and salt; Put the dough on a large round pan pizza and spread your fingers on the bottom. You can oven and a conventional rectangular pan.
4. Bake in preheated oven for 8 - 10 minutes, or until the dough is lightly browned. Slightly cool.
5. Beat the cream cheese with 1/2 cup sugar and vanilla.
6. Spread the filling over baked base.
7. Over filling beautifully arranged fruits and berries.

Mini Pizza Eggplant

Ingredients:

- 150 - 200 g of cheese
- 1 large onion
- Greens (any what you prefer)
- Salt and pepper to taste
- 3 eggplant (about 800 g)
- 400 g minced beef
- 3 tomatoes

Directions:

1. Eggplant cut into strips of 5 mm thick, sprinkle with salt and leave for at least 15 minutes. It's okay if they stand up any longer.

2. Sauté the onion and minced meat, adding salt to taste and pepper.
3. Tomatoes cut into circles. Finely chop the herbs.
4. Strips of eggplant dry with a paper towel and put on them: beef, tomato circles, sprinkle with grated cheese.
5. Put the pan with our work of culinary art in a preheated 200 ° C oven and bake for 20 - 30 minutes. Eggplant should be soft.
6. Remove the baking sheet from the oven and sprinkle with mini pizzas with finely chopped greens.

Broccoli-Bacon Skillet Pizza Recipe

Ingredients:

- 2/3 cup part-skim ricotta cheese

- 2 ounces parmigiano-reggiano cheese , grated (about 1/2 cup)

- 1 garlic clove , grated

- 1 tablespoon canola oil

- 10 ounces refrigerated whole-grain pizza dough

- 1 (12-ounce) package microwave-in-bag fresh broccoli florets

- 4 center-cut bacon slices, chopped

Directions:

1. Place dough upon counter at space temperature; cover to avoid drying.
2. Preheat broiler in order to high.
3. Microwave broccoli in accordance to package Directions:. Carefully open handbag; cool slightly. Halve or quarter bigger florets.
4. Cook bacon within a 10-inch cast-iron skillet over moderate heat 6 moments or until sharp; remove from skillet with a placed spoon.
5. Add spargelkohl to drippings within pan; toss nicely to coat. Eliminate broccoli from skillet.
6. Location cheeses and garlic clove inside a bowl; mix to blend (mixture is going to be thick).
7. Heat skillet over medium-high warmth. Roll dough in to a 10 1/2-inch circle.
8. Add essential oil to pan; beat to coat. Eliminate pan from warmth. Fit dough in to

pan, pressing somewhat up sides associated with pan.

9. Spread parmesan cheese mixture evenly more than dough.
10. Return skillet to medium-high warmth; cook 2 moments or until browned on bottom. Location pan in stove; broil 2 moments or until parmesan cheese is lightly browned.
11. Top pizza along with broccoli mixture; pan 1 minute.
12. Eliminate pan from stove; sprinkle bacon more than top. Cut in to 8 wedges.

Butternut Squash Pizza & White Sauce, Spinach, & Goat Cheese Recipe

Ingredients:

- 5 tablespoons refrigerated light alfredo sauce
- 1 teaspoon extra-virgin olive oil
- 6 cups fresh baby spinach
- 1 ounce goat cheese, crumbled (about 1/4 cup)
- 1/4 teaspoon freshly ground black pepper
- 2 cups precut peeled butternut squash (about 12 ounces)
- 1/4 teaspoon kosher salt, divided
- 1 (8-ounce) prebaked thin pizza crust (such as mama mary's)

Directions:

1. Preheat oven to 450°.
2. Place squash in a big microwave-safe dish; add water to a depth of 1/2 inch.
3. Cover with plastic wrap; microwave at HIGH 5 minutes.
4. Drain and toss squash with 1/8 teaspoon kosher salt.
5. While squash cooks, place pizza crust on a baking sheet; spread alfredo sauce over crust.
6. Heat oil in a nonstick skillet. Add spinach; sauté 1 minute. Stir in remaining 1/8 teaspoon salt.
7. Arrange wilted spinach over sauce.
8. Top with squash and goat cheese; sprinkle with pepper.
9. Bake pizza in bottom 3rd of oven at 450° for 6 minutes.
10. Turn oven to broil; cook pizza 1 additional minute or until crust is crispy.

11. Cut pizza into 8 wedges, and serve immediately.

Capricious Pizza

Ingredients:

- 1/2 cup mozzarella cheese, shredded
- 2 ounces very thin sliced prosciutto or boiled ham
- 1/2 cup mushrooms, sautéed
- 3 to 4 ounces of canned artichokes, well drained and sliced
- 1 pound of prepared pizza dough
- 1/2 cup pizza sauce of choice, more if desired
- 1/4 cup pureed or crushed tomatoes

Directions:

1. Preheat the oven and the pizza stone to 500 degrees for 30 minutes.

2. Arrange the pizza dough on a cookie sheet or a pizza peel that will allow transferring it to the stone when ready.
3. Spread the sauce over the dough evenly with the back of a spoon.
4. Top the dough with the mozzarella, prosciutto, mushrooms and artichokes.
5. Bake for 10 minutes or until the pizza is done. Let the pizza stand for 3 minutes before slicing to serve.

Fruited Brownie Pizza

Ingredients:

- 2 bananas, sliced into rounds

- 1 teaspoon lemon juice

- 1 1/2 cups sliced strawberries

- 1 kiwi fruit, peeled and sliced thinly

- 1/2 cup cleaned blueberries

- 8 ounces whipped topping, for serving

- 1 box of brownie mix

- 2 eggs

- 1/2 cup canola oil

- 1/4 cup water

- 8 ounces softened cream cheese

- 1/2 cup confectioner's sugar

Directions:

1. Prepare the brownie mix per package Directions: except cook on a pizza pan and spread to a 12-inch size. When finished, let cool completely.
2. Sprinkle the lemon juice over the banana slices to prevent turning colors.
3. Cream the confectioner's sugar and cream cheese together well.
4. Spread the cream cheese mixture evenly over the cooled brownie crust.
5. Arrange the fruit in whatever pattern or order desired to make an attractive presentation.
6. Slice into 12 wedges and serve each with a dollop of whipped topping.
7. You may also drizzle with chocolate syrup, if desired.

Italian Pizza On The Home Grill

Ingredients:

- 1 sweet pepper
- 1 eggplant
- 2 chicken sausages
- Handful of arugula
- 300 g of dough for pizza
- 150 g tomato sauce
- 100 g of mozzarella cheese
- Olive oil

Directions:

1. Eggplant cut into circles, pepper strips. Grate the cheese on a large grater.

2. Grease the grill with olive oil and fry it on both sides of the pepper and eggplant.
3. Roll out the dough thinly.
4. Put the dough on the surface, where the vegetables were fried, and cook it at a high temperature for 3-5 minutes under a closed lid. Turn over.
5. Grease the dough with tomato sauce, sprinkle with cheese. put the eggplant, pepper on top.
6. Cook at high temperature for another 3-5 minutes under a closed lid.
7. Then reduce the temperature in half and cook for 5 minutes under a closed lid.

Homemade Pizza

Ingredients:

- Salt 1 tsp

- Sugar 1 tsp.

- Olive oil 1 tablespoon

- Sauce:

- Garlic, chop 2 cloves

- Olive oil 4 tablespoons

- Canned diced tomato 1 jar

- Flour, durum wheat, 250 g

- Dry yeast 2 tsp

- Basil leaves handful

- Salt and pepper

Directions:

1. Mix flour, yeast, salt, sugar, 1 tablespoon of olive oil and 180-200 ml of warm water.
2. Knead the elastic dough; cover and leave for proofing for 1 hour.
3. Fry garlic in 4 tablespoons of olive oil, then add tomatoes, Basil, salt and pepper.
4. Heat a grill or barbecue pan. Roll 4 balls of dough, roll each into a flat cake.
5. Grease from one side with oil and cook greased side down, 2-4 minutes.
6. Oil the other side, turn the cake over and fry. Repeat with the remaining flatbreads.
7. Brush the finished cakes with sauce liberally and add the toppings according to your taste

Pizza With Seafood

Ingredients:

- Bell pepper 30 g.

- Mozzarella cheese 150 g.

- Worcestershire sauce 2 tablespoons

- Soy sauce (crab) 2 tablespoons

- Honey 100 g.

- Dr pepper's drink 100 g.

- Rum dark 80 g.

- Cumin ground 1 teaspoon

- Tabasco sauce

- Tiger prawns 3 pcs.

- Mussels 2 pcs.
- Octopus 2 pcs.
- Cuttlefish (mini) 2 pcs.
- Salmon 50 g.
- Ground paprika 1 tablespoon

Directions:

1. Let's start with the dough. To do this, sift the flour, add dry yeast, salt, sugar, oil and warm water.
2. The dough is placed in a bag and leave to approach.
3. Cooking barbecue sauce. To do this, mix all the Ingredients: and bring to a boil.
4. Get a lot of sauce from these Ingredients:. It can be poured into a bottle and use if necessary.
5. Stretch the dough to a diameter of 30 cm.

6. Grease barbecue sauce, put vegetables, cheese, seafood, send in a heated grill, which is preheated stone for pizza.
7. Bake on the grill with the lid closed.
8. Decorate with arugula, capers on a twig, sprinkled with olive oil.

www.ingramcontent.com/pod-product-compliance
Lightning Source LLC
LaVergne TN
LVHW010219070526
838199LV00062B/4652